girl
boner
Journal

AUGUST McLAUGHLIN

girl
boher
Journal

*A Guided Journal
to Sexual Joy and
Empowerment*

AMBERJACK
PUBLISHING

Amberjack Publishing
1472 E. Iron Eagle Drive
Eagle, Idaho 83616
http://amberjackpublishing.com

The author of this book does not dispense medical advice or prescribe the use of any technique as a form of treatment for physical, emotional, or medical problems without the advice of a physician, either directly or indirectly. This book is written as a source of information only. The information contained in this book should by no means be considered a substitute for the advice of a qualified medical professional, who should always be consulted with questions regarding a person's health.

All efforts have been made to ensure the accuracy of the information contained in this book as of the date published. The publisher and author disclaim liability for any adverse effects that may occur as a result of applying the methods suggested in this book.

The personal events of the author's life contained herein are accurate to the best of the author's memory. Minor details which do not impact the story have been changed as necessary to protect the privacy of those involved. August McLaughlin owns the Girl Boner® trademark.

Publisher's Cataloging-in-Publication data
Names: McLaughlin, August, author.
Title: Girl boner journal : a guided journal to sexual joy and empowerment / by August McLaughlin.
Description: Idaho : Amberjack Publishing, [2018]
Identifiers: LCCN 2018037002 | ISBN 9781948705219 (pbk. : alk. paper)
Subjects: LCSH: Women--Sexual behavior. | Diaries--Authorship.
Classification: LCC HQ29 .M4649 2018 | DDC 306.7082--dc23 LC record available at https://lccn.loc.gov/2018037002

ISBN: 978-1-948705-21-9

Cover Design: Blue Cup Creative

This journal belongs to

_____

Introduction

THE THING ABOUT SOUL TRUTHS

"ARE YOU THE LADY with the vagina show?"

I spun around to see someone who could have been a friend of my grandmother, with the tight white curls framing her 'I just baked you cookies' face. Only no one in Grandma E's circles would have said "vagina," much less approached someone who did so frequently. I was leaving the studio after recording an episode of my podcast, *Girl Boner Radio*, and while I was accustomed to interesting exchanges with passersby on the Hollywood streets afterward, this felt unusual.

"Yes, that's me," I replied with a smile, aware that no one else at the studio hosted a show with vaginal leanings.

"Well keep doing it. Girls could never talk about that stuff in my day. Do you have a light?"

The woman was full of surprises. "I don't. But I do have a sex toy!"

I'm not sure what compelled me to the pull the vibrator I'd featured in the day's episode out of my purse, but when the woman looked at me straight-faced for a moment, I wondered if her warmth for me had expired.

"If it's new . . . I'll take it!"

Thank goddesses. As we continued chatting, I learned that she was born and raised in Miami, where I had lived for two years before moving to Los Angeles.

"Ah, South Beach, señorita! I could see you spreading the news about sex there. Bet you fit right in."

"Actually, not at all," I told her. I'd started on my sexual empowerment path by then, but far more learning and growing remained before all-things-Girl Boner would unfold. Then I shared what helped me along more than most anything: not a sex toy or spicy conversation, but my journal, some java, and a pen.

It was a rare cool morning in South Beach, Miami, and I was scribbling away in my journal between sips of Cuban coffee, its richness equaling the intensity of my outpour. Writing, writing, writing . . . *fast*. Free-writing several pages each morning was a practice I'd taken up while reading *The Artist's Way*, by Julia Cameron, a book I'd hoped would help me crack the conundrum I had found myself in: *"I should be so happy. But I'm not."*

I had a caring partner who'd begun to find his professional footing. I'd been promoted to deputy editor at a magazine and was finally able to cut back on the several-at-once jobs I'd been juggling to support us. And after rocky stints of semi-homelessness, we had a place of our own, a studio apartment that could well have been a mansion, given my "Oh my gosh, it has walls!" adoration. I'd even saved up enough cash beyond our monthly necessities to sign up for the acting class I'd longed to take since our arrival, Miami being a stepping stone to the acting mecca of Los Angeles. Things were finally on-track; the leap we'd taken to move there, with little more than $300 and whatever belongings we could fit into several suit-cases, was paying off. Gone were the "Why don't you just come back to Minnesota?" comments from well-intentioned friends who'd offered to introduce us to so-and-so at such-and-such company back home. We had said we would figure things out and we had.

So what was with this unsettled feeling? The vague sensation swirled in me like the first hint of nausea before a flu. Every morning, I awoke to it, in that half-asleep state before you're lured from your innermost wonderings.

"It'll pass," I told myself at first. But after days, weeks, and then months, it didn't. Was there something wrong with me?

I don't know why this experience felt so different from the many times I'd assumed that yes, actually, there *was* something wrong with me. Perhaps it was the growth-work I'd done to move past an eating disorder and embrace my sexuality. Or the fact that both had allowed me to rec-ognize my dream of an acting career. Dreams do have a way of inspiring confidence and unstoppable motivation. Or maybe emerging from survival mode helped most. I no longer felt frantic; I had space to feel.

Whatever the reasons, I decided that this time I would not let the unsettled swirl go untapped. I wouldn't attempt to diet or exercise or mentally bully the feelings away. This time, I would unleash them. Little did I imagine that in doing so, I would end up unleashing more of myself.

So on that crisp morning with sunlight hitting my coffee and a pen clutched in my hand, when I saw the word "divorce" spill onto the page, I trusted it.

Oh . . . Yes. That.

The answer I'd been seeking had revealed itself, settling my swirly upset like an antacid. Journaling freely helped me see what I'd resisted: cracks in my relationship that no amount of heart-to-hearts or therapy could fix. I began to see that I'd married someone to avoid aloneness and for the ways he once assuaged my lingering insecurities as I traded one set of dependencies for another. But I'd grown since then. Now I felt trapped in a conglomeration of creative work for others and taking care of others' needs in lieu of my own.

That morning I realized that if I wished to live authentically and make my wildest dreams come true, including those I had yet to perceive, I would have to go out on my own. Only then would I begin to find and fulfill my life's purpose. While facing many questions that I couldn't yet answer, I had no doubt about this one.

As galvanizing as this realization was, it was also petrifying, perhaps the way parents feel holding a newborn, hoping they won't screw this fragile miracle up. Moving forward would require difficult conversations, hurting loved ones, undergoing others' judgment, and maintaining faith amid so very many unknowns. The last time I'd gone out on my own, I'd landed at death's doorstep, cloaked in nightmares that would take years to shake.

Can I really do this? By the time the question occurred to me, it wasn't a question at all. That's the thing about soul truths. Once we embrace them, they become virtually undeniable.

The next weeks and months were at times excruciating, but they also held some of the most exhilarating and invaluable experiences of my life. For every loss and hardship, I gained manifold rewards: a closer relationship with my mom, kindred friendships, my first paid acting roles, a sense of freedom and realness I'd never before known.

The next year, in the same journal, as a hurricane raged outside the apartment I shared with a roommate, I listed out my biggest aspirations, including a move to Los Angeles. Once I'd increased my financial cushion by 3,000 dollars, I promised myself, I would book my ticket. During a visit to see my parents in Minnesota not long after, I learned I had booked a job for a California-based company. It would pay 3,000 dollars exactly, and it would include a few billboards. Even before I officially moved to Los Angeles, I was there. Or, at least, my face was.

As you know if you've read my book *Girl Boner: The Good Girl's Guide to Sexual Empowerment*, this move would end up playing significant roles in my sexual journey, furthering my way to all-things-Girl Boner, this journal included. Releasing thoughts I scarcely realized I'd had on paper set me on a path rich with pleasure and meaning. It revealed so much about myself and my desires, allowing me to face and embrace, rather than avoid or ignore, inclinations to live bolder, go after my dreams, and even masturbate for the first time. I'm not suggesting that through journaling, you too will end up getting divorced, switching careers, and moving across the country where you'll have a life-changing orgasm. But I do think there's little better method than journaling to peel back the layers in any area for which we desire growth, our sexual selves included.

Journaling has a way of unmasking parts of ourselves we've hidden, lost touch with, or learned to neglect. This is why I consider the medium invaluable when it comes to embracing our authentic sexuality and pleasure of all kinds. In a world in which women, LGBTQIA+, and non-binary folks are shunned for seeming "too sexual," sexual in the "wrong ways," or "not sexual enough" and our pleasure too easily falls to the wayside, journaling is basically a superpower.

When we journal our hearts—and our Girl Boners—out, we're able to connect with our truest selves, our deepest longings, our grandest hopes, and our most daunting fears, without concern over others' criticism or opinions. If we wish to contribute to a better world and lead deeply gratifying lives, whether in or outside of the metaphorical bedroom, I believe this kind of authenticity is a prerequisite. (As delicious frosting, clearing the "gunk" from your mind can make sex more pleasurable and relationships of all kinds far groovier.)

If I'd had a journal such as this early on in my own sexual empowerment journey, I have no doubt that I would've learned to thrive much sooner. I'm so honored to play some small part in yours.

All my love,

August

HOW TO USE THIS BOOK

THERE'S NO WRONG WAY to keep a journal, *Girl Boner Journal* included. Consider the following methods or use one of your own conjuring, whatever makes the most sense for you. Then throughout, use the prompts and questions as your guide, giving yourself full freedom to write in any direction you wish.

SUGGESTED METHODS:

As you read *Girl Boner: The Good Girl's Guide to Sexual Empowerment.* In many ways, I've followed the basic arc of *Girl Boner* for this book's content, to make journaling as you read a breeze. Use this book to take the journaling prompts in *Girl Boner* deeper, dedicating the most energy to topics that resonate with you.

On its own, at your desired pace. If you've already read *Girl Boner* or want to use this journal on its own, start from the beginning and move along at your desired pace.

By topic or theme. If you would prefer to jump around, or if you're going through something specific and wish to journal accordingly, consider journaling by topic or theme. Skim over the index to entries, then choose whatever heading most strikes you on any given day.

Book club style. Girl Boner gab makes just about everything more fun—not that I'm biased *at all.* Consider working this book into gatherings of like-minded friends.

In tandem with therapy. You can also use the exercises to address or select topics you hope to cover in therapy with the guidance of a professional. (Please do seek professional support for any issue you struggle to manage on your own. There's never any shame, only beauty and courage, in that.)

STYLE IDEAS

Circle and flow. If you're new to journaling and not quite sure where to start, circle the question or prompt you'd like to write about in each section. Reiterate it in the first line, then complete it using your own words, for as few or many sentences as you'd like. If desired, repeat this process for additional prompts.

For example, if the prompt were to say, "What's your favorite color and why?" you'd write "My favorite color is . . ." then continue writing from there.

Pour it all out. Using the prompts as inspiration, let your thoughts spill out onto the page. Free-write without concern over grammar or prose. This can be especially helpful if you feel a bit stuck, feel overwhelmed by a slew of thoughts and feelings, or tend to struggle with perfectionism.

Doodle or sketch. Are you more of a doodler than a scribbler? If so, or the notion sounds fun, draw or color your responses. Create colorful word collages or cartoons. Literally cut and paste images or text from old magazines or newspapers onto pages if you wish.

Fictionalize or dialogue it. You don't have to have particular writing skills to hone an impactful journaling practice. (In fact, overthinking how "good" you're writing can stand in the way of self-discovery, inviting a sense of self-consciousness.) If you love writing or feel a bit uncomfortable with IRL stories, let those creative juices run wild through short stories or poems.

Mix and match. Are you a perpetual free spirit who can't help but bend the "rules?" (High fives. I feel you!) Let yourself choose between the above methods for each section, guiding with your mood and instincts on any given day.

TIPS AND TRICKS

Keep journaling convenient by storing your *Girl Boner Journal* in a place you visit routinely, such as your nightstand.

If you're out and about without your journal and feel the urge to write, email notes to yourself or jot thoughts down on paper to transfer later.

Center yourself before writing with a few slow, deep breaths, with your eyes closed if desired.

Use a special pen you love.

Consider free-writing upon waking, especially if you go with pouring it all out.

Give yourself grace o' plenty. Be gentle with yourself, aiming to do your best rather than aiming for "perfection."

Exercise One

STARTING WHERE YOU ARE

"And the day came when the risk to remain tight in a bud was more painful than the risk it took to blossom."

—Elizabeth Appell (frequently attributed to Anaïs Nin)

———————————

NO MATTER WHERE YOU are on your Girl Boner journey, I promise you it's a beautiful and worthy place—to begin, to continue, or to start anew. With a pen in hand, let the words flow to the page without judgment. Be kind to yourself. Stay open. Now, ready, set . . . begin.

How do you define your sexuality? I believe our sexuality is inherent in all we do and who we are. It's in the air we breathe, the words we speak, the ways we interact with others, and how we connect intimately with our bodies, sensuality, and selves. Perhaps you prefer to define your sexuality in terms of orientation, relationship style, the ways you express your sexual desires, or experience erotic sensations. There is no right or wrong answer.

How do you feel about your sexuality now? How would you *like* to feel?

Example: *I'm feeling really . . . confused? Excited? Curious? Okay, and I'm also a little nervous. I guess you could say I'm basically happy with my sexuality, as in my sex life. But I know there's more to it than that. I would really like to feel more confident and sure about _____ and _____, but I also feel proud of myself for starting this journal. DEEP BREATH. Here I go.*

What ten adjectives would you use to describe your sex life or how you feel about your sexuality lately?

What book or movie title would you use to describe your sex life?

Exercise Two

RECALLING SEX ED

"YOU COULD HANG A backpack on that thing." That's literally what I recall thinking as I sat in that awkward class known as sex ed as a medical drawing of a person with an erect penis glowed on the projector screen. I felt an odd mix of curious, perplexed, and ripped off as we learned a pleasurable fact or two about guys and zilch for girls or women. Were bleeding, cramps, and STDs really all I had to look forward to? Thankfully, no. But it took me years to figure that out.

Imagine if you'd learned as little about basic English, math, or reading as you did about sex and sexuality growing up. No doubt, you'd face challenges when attempting to type emails, manage a budget, or devour books. A lack of sex education can function the same way.

If you're a curious self-learner, you probably raced off to gather what you could about sexuality from whatever resources you could find. Or maybe you learned about all things sexual through gossip, hearsay, sex-positive parents, or eventually, experience. These formative happenings don't define us, but they do influence our journeys.

What did you first learn about sex and sexuality, and how?

What was the first negative message you recall learning?

How about the first positive?

How did these messages make you feel?

How do they show up in your life now?

Exercise Three

REAL TALK ABOUT PERIODS

I'M GOING TO TAKE a not-so-wild guess that bleeding, cramps, or oth-er-things-menstrual came up for you in your sex ed recollections. Am I right? While sex ed tends to bypass pleasure, there's seldom a shortage of period talk. In light of it, most people feel more fear or dread than empowerment. So before we dive further into sexy spice and more, let's have a quick visit with Aunt Flo.

How do you feel about menstruation? Have you bought into the myth—which is easy to do—that PMS or periods make a person "crazy"? Cramps, bleeding, and mood swings aren't necessarily fun, and sometimes symptoms are downright debilitating. (If the latter is true for you, please see your doctor or seek support from a free clinic, if possible.) But they are a natural part of being a person with a uterus, and not as "yuck" worthy as you might have thought back in sex ed. For many people, they bring groovy benefits.

It's also important to note that having access to menstrual products and healthcare is a privilege countless people lack. Around the world, menstruating youth miss or even drop out of school due to period shame, which also keeps far too many from seeking treatment for potentially serious related medical conditions. And menstruation for people living on the streets can feel catastrophic, yet tampons, pads, and menstrual cups aren't terribly common donations at shelters.

For those of us who menstruate, moving past pervasive stigmas and embracing our cycles or empowering ourselves to address any related health issues can invite awesome advantages. Many people feel more creative, strong, or attuned with themselves leading up to Aunt Flo's stay, and a glorious sense of renewal once the bleeding starts or stops. (*Ah, spring has sprung!*) Some folks find period sex especially pleasurable, consider orgasm powerful cramps busters, prefer a sex-break while menstruating, or enjoy the added arousal ovulation brings. No matter how you feel about sex and periods, it's all good.

I personally see PMS as a magnifying glass that sheds light on important issues I might not otherwise address, which can pave the way to more pleasure and less stress. The more intensely we feel, the more likely we are to act. So before periods, we might have an easier time standing up for ourselves or others, making the hormonal shifts a powerful tool we can rely on. Chipping away at period shame can even help minimize menstrual symptoms, or at least make them less daunting, and make us more likely to seek any needed medical care. Similarly, sexual empowerment and embracing our bodies can bring a whole new respect for menstrual cycles.

No matter your stance, write a poem about periods. Or let your thoughts about menstruating, well, flow!

What kind of pleasure can you experience leading up to or during your or a partner's periods?

How do you feel about period sex?

Exercise Four

GIRL BONER TURNING POINTS

YOU'RE GOING ABOUT YOUR life as usual when something pretty wondrous happens. An epiphany strikes—a truth, a realization. While you look the same from the outside, except perhaps for a newfound glow, you feel somehow . . . changed. It's as though a blank sky has revealed its stars, asking *who are you now?* Or perhaps it says, *YES, finally. This is who I've always been.*

One of mine took place at age thirty, the first time I delved into solo play. Before then, I'd spent years leaping from relationship to relationship (or hookup to hookup, for a stint), all the while assuming my sexual needs were met—so why even consider masturbation? That all changed one lonely night when I decided to act on my sexual urges. Just me, myself, and a hot-pink dildo. As I shared in Girl Boner, *the experience turned out to be as steamy as it was life-shifting. In the afterglow of the resultant big O, it dawned on me that I'd viewed my sexuality as dependent on another person, versus first and foremost my own. And wow, did that make a powerful difference. I've not only experienced far more pleasure since then but learned a great deal about my body and desires.*

Girl Boner turning points can happen at any stage of life, on any day, and in a single moment. Maybe it was your first time experiencing orgasm or locating your G-spot, or the time you realized that you're attracted to people of various genders, or asexual, or queer.

Write about such a moment. What did it teach you?

Exercise Five

WHEN THE TRUTH HURTS

"The truth will set you free, but first it will piss you off."
  —Activist battle cry

WHEN MY FRIEND JJ realized she was into BDSM well into her forties, she texted me, sounding a bit upset: "I spent a decade married and hating my sex life. What if I had figured this out early on?" My own specifics were different, but I understood where she was coming from.

I'll never forget the college class in which the professor prompted a discussion about sex, the one that set me on my sexual discovery quest. Amid my giddy lightbulb stir, I felt angry. Realizing I'd been carrying sexual shame around for years—so much so, I hadn't really even *talked* about sex—meant that I'd have to tap into the shame's consequences. Like JJ, I'd have to dig into daunting questions about myself, my sexuality, and the world, wondering how my life would have been different, "if only . . ." I'd have to walk into dens of trolls and my own dark closets. And I'd have to analyze and sit with heartbreaking systemic problems if I wished to make any sort of lasting change. Meanwhile, I began to recognize and grieve all I'd lost.

It's okay to feel anger, frustration, and hurt related to epiphanies and the growth efforts they inspire. Let your feelings OUT! Yell them if you wish or blast them down onto the page in bold, dark letters. Give them air, so they don't fester. The more you let yourself experience rather than resist painful emotions, the quicker they'll morph into fabulous fuel and the sooner you'll find hope and healing.

Exercise Six

YOUR SEXY PARTS

"I had a feeling that Pandora's box contained the mysteries of woman's sensuality, so different from a man's and for which man's language was so inadequate. The language of scx had yet to be invented. The language of the senses was yet to be explored."

—Anaïs Nin, *Delta of Venus*

SAM, A WRITER IN Los Angeles, told me she has early memories of "looking down [there]." Naturally flexible, she caught occasional glimpses of her vulva while bending this way or that as a child. Around age fifteen, she was applying makeup at a bathroom vanity in the nude, her feet propped in the sink, when she noticed far more than the outside of her genitals in a mirrored medicine cabinet.

"It was a lot of information to take in unexpectedly," she said. "The interior looked different, more exotic than its outer parts, but it was me. It wasn't as 'pretty' as expected. The assemblage was more complex than 'pretty' typically allows for. But, after my surprise, I understood that it was me. The most delicate, vulnerable part of me. The part I would share with only those I thought special enough. At least, then, that's what I believed."

Decades later, she finds it fascinating that vulvas and all they encompass remain largely taboo. We can freely talk about our breast appearance and health, she noted, but our genitals?

When I asked SAM what she would tell someone who feels daunted by the notion of taking a good look at their genital region, she said, "Look at it. Appreciate it. Embrace it. Love it. It's your external heart. It is the part of you that is most powerful and most vulnerable. See its wonder and respect it."

If you have a vulva—which includes labia (lips), the vaginal opening, the opening to the urethra (where you pee from), and clitoris—you probably grew up with some amount of genital mystique, which is a fancy way of saying, *What the heck is going on down there?* Or maybe you were one of the lucky ones who learned proper terms like *vulva*, *vagina*, and *clitoris*. No matter your genital specifics, spend some time exploring and celebrating your sexy parts.

How do you feel about your genitals?

If you've looked "down there," describe the experience(s).

Exercise Seven

ODE TO YOUR GENITALS

THE TERMS WE USE to describe our genitals can say a lot about our perceptions of them. Sadly, there's no shortage of negative descriptors and many, many people feel shame or confusion when it comes to the actual anatomical terms. While it's a good idea to have a basic understanding of these words (find them all in *Girl Boner*, Chapter Three), positive nicknames are fine, too.

I asked my newsletter subscribers what they call their own or a partner's genitals and the answers were, well, revealing! Here are just a few of their replies:

"Pussy"

"Cock"

"My friends. So we can be friendly."

"My pretty pink parts because I used to not embrace my womanhood and wouldn't even look at mine. Once I embraced who I was, this name fit for me."

"I've always thought it'd be great to call my vulva Lola after the Barry Manilow song: 'Her name was Lola, she was a showgirl . . .'"

"Pricilla"

"'pussy' for female genitalia, though we've had to work to reclaim the word after a certain groper grabbed it. I like 'cock' for his penis, as 'penis' is a bit clinical. But I will say we now use both boy boner and girl boner!"

The clitoris is the only organ whose sole function is pleasure. That doesn't make it superior to the penis, but it does make it equally groovy. As we explored in *Girl Boner*, the clitoris and penis are anatomical equivalents. Derived from the same genetic material, they both expand during arousal (yay, Boners!) and set the stage for intense pleasure. Some intersex people have ambiguous genitalia, such as a very large clitoris or tiny penis, also derived from this material.

Describe your clitoris, penis, or another genital part. Write it a fan letter or love poem. If you wish, write one for a partner's precious part as well.

What words have you, or a partner(s), used to describe your genitals over the years?

Are these keeper terms or would you like for them to change?

Exercise Eight
PERMISSION TO WANT

Hey, gorgeous gal. You're allowed to desire and seek pleasures of the flesh. Your wants and fantasies are valid.

I WAS IN MY mid-twenties and decidedly single after a spree of serious relationships when I gave myself permission to (really, really) want. After telling my then agent that a glamorous night I'd spent on the town surrounded by sexy actors had ended with me alone in my pajamas with a bowl of Cheerios, he seemed surprised: "You know you could have had any one of them, right?"

Um. What? Did he mean . . . sex?!?

I wasn't so sure he was right about the actors, but that he had expected I would get busy with someone I barely knew for the sheer fun of it really got me thinking. "Good girl" me could actually have had—dare I say it—*Casual Sex?*

The next time I entered a nightclub, having given my Girl Boner free reign, I wasn't just interested in sex. Want nearly became me. Shortly after, it struck me that I'd experienced the sort of permission men receive from an early age and in myriad ways to freely and shamelessly desire sex.

Do you give yourself permission to want? Yes, I'm talking about sex, but not *only* sex. When we give ourselves the go-ahead to desire sexual pleasure to our Girl Boners' content, pleasure throughout our lives can increase, along with the potency of our orgasms. We can also experience the near opposite, when feeling turned off in life sends our Girl Boner into hiding. Understanding our desires—and whether or not we wish to allow and nurture them—can carry us far, from the bedroom to the boardroom.

What pleasures have you allowed yourself to indulge in lately?

When you notice sexual desire, do you find ways to act on it? Or do you consistently distract yourself from it, allowing other priorities to take hold?

If you do tend to embrace your desires, how has doing so influenced your life?

Exercise Nine

MISMATCHED LIBIDOS

"As women, we're told the story, to 'keep it in your pants' until you meet Prince Charming, then it should all magically work. What I realize now is, I had 'kept it in my pants' for so many years, that it wasn't really reasonable for things to work once I met someone I cared about."

—Pam Costa

PAM'S JOURNEY, DETAILED FURTHER in *Girl Boner*, began when she realized her otherwise happy marriage felt strained by her low sex drive, setting her on a path of self-discovery. Any guess what she learned? That she's a bodacious goddess who happens to desire more sex than she'd realized, beneath layers of shaming messages she'd absorbed all her life.

So many factors can fuel libido decline, in people of all gender identities. While desiring sex seldom, rarely, or never is perfectly fine if *you* are okay with it, I frequently hear from folks who wish they desired sex more. They want to want to engage in sexy play, but something seems off. And that is a perfect place to start seeking solutions: with awareness of your wishes and a willingness to move toward them.

The same can apply if you tend to experience higher-than-their (a partner's) sex drive. Since covering the topic on my blog, I hear from women routinely who feel either frustrated and concerned or somehow defective for wanting more sex than a partner. When mismatched libido becomes a source of tension in a relationship, it's well worth addressing.

If you're experiencing lower-than-you'd-like libido, what seems to be standing in the way? Write freely about each potential barrier, then create a list of action steps you could take to address them. (If you're not sure of the cause, review *Girl Boner*, Chapter Four.)

If you're regularly on the higher end libido-wise, how does that make you feel? What efforts to address this, if any, seem worthwhile?

Exercise Ten

TITILLATING TURN-ONS

Whatever sets your soul on fire is valid and embraceable.

MY FRIEND B'S FAVORITE turn-on is toast. Yes, the crunchy bread. "I love the smell of it, its crispiness, its flavor," she's told me, adding that salted butter is a must. (So noted!) And when she wants to rev up the Girl Boner heat? You guessed it. She often heads to the toaster when she feels, or wants to feel, aroused.

"I suppose it doesn't take an expert to figure out that it's because my first partner and I used to eat toast after having sex," she said of the probable reason. "Funnily enough, I don't even miss or think about that person or the sex, but the toast thing stuck. And hey, it's pretty cheap and easy for a go-to, right?"

On the other hand, common turn-ons such as porn and vibrators don't do much for her. B gave up on trying to get aroused by such things, she said, because "why try and be somebody you're not?"

Many other folks find kissing, sensual touch, eye-locking with a lover, watching spicy films, or reading erotic stories the most titillating. Still others have fetishes, like foot fervor, or they fantasize about being dominated or dominating someone else. And to B's point, they're all worthy.

What turns you on the most lately?

What turns you on when you're alone versus with a partner?

What have you felt *"should"* turn you on, but simply doesn't?

Write yourself a permission slip to desire or not desire whatever the heck you want!

Exercise Eleven

CHOOSING YOUR TURN-ONS

"What turns us on (or off) is learned from culture, in much the same way children learn vocabulary and accents from culture."

—Emily Nagoski, *Come as You Are: The Surprising New Science that Will Transform Your Sex Life*

———————————

DID YOU KNOW THAT there are cultures in which women's breasts aren't considered any sexier than, say, their elbows or ears? In various populations around the world and throughout history, women's ankles, hair, and feet are deemed more erotic. Similarly, in some modern cultures, straight women prefer men with hairless chests, and the color pink is considered "manly."

It takes effort, but we can shift our perceptions of what tickles our Girl Boners, should we wish to. Here's a true example: Shen H., a grad student in Seattle, was really into extra-large penises. Her first boyfriend had a large one, and she grew to relish being filled up (and then some). She began watching porn featuring well-endowed performers as the aesthetics became her fetish and passion.

Then one day she met Rob at a cafe where she worked as a barista. This tall, burly guy ignited her like no one else had. When they had sex for the first time, Shen was "admittedly horrified" to discover that Rob's penis was substantially smaller than any she'd seen. Over time and with plentiful effort, namely challenging her beliefs and "looking to find hotness in different imagery and ideas," she grew to adore Rob's member.

"I've experienced pleasure in ways I had never thought I could," she said, adding that even her fantasies have changed. "I'm now an all-size opportunity lover."

Create a list of your top turn-ons. When did you realize you find each one sexy?

Are there any turn-ons you'd like to change?

What societal depiction of "sexy" irritates you most, and why?

Exercise Twelve

GIRL BONER BUZZKILLS

You know what lowers many women's libido? Inequality. Repression. Damaging myths. When women rise, so do Girl Boners.

UNDERSTANDING WHAT MAKES YOUR sex drive come to a halt can be just as important as understanding your turn-ons. As I explore in *Girl Boner*, inequality, misogyny, and demeaning myths are at the root of *so many* turn-offs for women and femmes. We also addressed other biggies, such as stress, depression, anxiety, sleep deficiency, restrictive dieting, sexual pain, and a history of sexual trauma.

One common byproduct of feeling frequently turned off (or even less sex-enthused than you'd like) due to any of these factors is undue shame. Trust me, if these perceivable roadblocks are tinkering with your sexual desire you are far from alone, not even a little bit broken, and worth every ounce of support and care. People and messages that make you feel less-than or that interfere with your access to worthy support is the problem, not you. And a bit of awareness can go a long way.

(For practical ways to start addressing these buzzkills, head to *Girl Boner*, Chapter Four.)

Write about a time in your life when you felt deeply respected and cared for. How did it influence your sexuality?

What types of emotional labor stand in the way of Girl Boner bliss? If you weren't expected to be "nice" in response to harassment, censor your thoughts or feelings, or take care of most of the housework, for example, would you feel more lively?

Create a list of your turn-offs, whether deep or more superficial (those are okay, too!). What would *for sure* keep you from enjoying time with a date or friend or feeling in the mood for sex?

Exercise Thirteen

YOUR BODY, TURNED ON

"To feel aroused is to feel alive. Having great sex is like taking in huge lungfuls of fresh air, essential to your body, essential to your health, and essential to your life."

—Fiona Thrust, *Naked and Sexual*

BLUSHING, SWELLING, ARCHING, TINGLING . . . We all experience arousal uniquely, though there are definitely common threads.

How does your body experience turn-on? Create a list or describe a specific experience, going into as much detail as you like.

In case you could use some inspiration, here are a few survey responses I received:

"A sense of warmth and well being, like eating a bowl of soup, only all over my body."

"My body experiences turn-on with swelling and wetness."

"Pulse races, breathe rapidly, I get moist (because that is everyone's favorite word!)."

"It feels like electricity in my veins and my lady parts start to throb!"

"Vaginal wetness, accelerated heartbeat, increased blood flow to clit and labia, fidgety, increased focus on achieving an orgasm as soon as possible."

"Initially as a tightening of the scrotum"

"Less immediate wetness at age 57, but it does come eventually, no pun intended. Definitely swelling!"

"Sparkly Christmas lights"

Exercise Fourteen

DIFFERENT TYPES OF 'GASMS

You deserve love, laughter, and mind-blowing orgasms.

THERE ARE MANY WAYS to experience orgasm and a plethora of types to be had. I'm all for getting off for the sake of it, but some of the best climaxes take us somewhat by surprise. We aren't merely beelining toward it so much as savoring our way to its allowance.

Susanna Brisk, aka the Sexual Intuitive®, took this notion to a whole new level. While some people train themselves to experience orgasm through thoughts alone (the think-gasms, discussed in Chapter Five of *Girl Boner*), Susanna was cruising along the highway when one happened.

"I was thinking about somebody and I just was like, 'Oh my goodness!'" she told me. "I had to pull over. And then once I knew how to do it, then it became almost like a hobby."

Even so, Susanna feels it's important to note that there is no superior way to enjoy orgasmic pleasure. You aren't sexually inferior if you can't "think yourself off," as some of her students have perceived, or superior if you can. In her work, Susanna helps people uncover what turns them on the most, without analyzing it or being attached to any result. "Once you have a strong energetic connection between your Cerebral, Emotional, and Genital, there are no limitations to how much pleasure you can give and receive," she said.

No two orgasms are identical, and there is no "best" way to experience one. Whether you rely on your fingers, toys, a penis, or your thoughts alone to invite orgasmic bliss, you deserve that kind of pleasure.

Do you tend to experience orgasm deep inside, externally, or a mix of both?

Describe your most unique or surprising orgasm.

If you haven't experienced orgasm, what do you imagine it would feel like?

Have you ever faked an orgasm? Why or why not?

Exercise Fifteen

SEXY SOLO PLAY

"We have reason to believe that man first walked upright to free his [her/their] hands for masturbation."

—Lily Tomlin, actress, comedian, writer, and producer

ISABELLE KOHN SAYS SHE masturbates "weird," and she knows it for two reasons. The sex journalist, educator, and coach has never seen anyone else go about it in such a way and people seem "genuinely bemused" when she describes it like this:

"I lay on my right side, and place my left palm on my clit. Then I use my hips to grind on my palm, which sort of kneads or massages my clit without moving much. I can't do it the other way around—left side, right hand—and I can't do it on my back. I also can't get off with my fingers—it *has* to be my palm, unless it's during the two or three times a year I'm inconsolably horny, in which case pretty much anything will make me come."

While she can speak freely about this now, Isabelle long felt too ashamed to. When someone would attempt to touch her clitoris in a way others seem to love, it did nothing for her, but guiding them to her liking would have felt embarrassing. That all changed when she solo-played her way to an orgasm so strong, she said it literally knocked her out for five hours.

"When I woke up, [I] was full of energy and this weird electric optimism," she recalled. "In fact, I was feeling so good I knocked out an entire

2,000 word article in a few hours. It was *good*, too. At that point, I realized that if I was capable of doing that to my body just from getting off in the offbeat way I do, it didn't matter *how* I did it, just that it happened. I felt pretty cool after that."

No matter your technique, masturbation is a natural, beautiful way to get better acquainted with our bodies, prioritize pleasure and self-care, and invite the many groovy perks of orgasm, from reduced stress and better sleep to a shinier appearance and outlook.

What's your favorite way to engage in *ménage à moi*?

What's the most unique or creative solo-play experience you recall?

If you tend to go about masturbation the same way every time, how could you change things up on occasion?

If you're not into solo play, what other practice do you prefer for sexual expression or release?

Exercise Sixteen

ORAL SEX SEXINESS

"She arches her body like a cat on a stretch. She nuzzles her cunt into my face like a filly at the gate. She smells of the sea. She smells of rockpools when I was a child. She keeps a starfish in there. I crouch down to taste the salt, to run my fingers around the rim. She opens and shuts like a sea anemone. She's refilled each day with fresh tides of longing."

—Jeanette Winterson, *Written on the Body*

HOW DO YOU FEEL about oral sex? While giving or receiving it is many people's cuppa, it's so-so or unappealing for others. Los Angeles-based author Beverly Diehl falls into the first category, as long as they aren't combined in 69 formation, which she finds too distracting.

"I have had sensations so intense when receiving, I've experienced synesthesia," she said, which involves "almost hallucinogenic visions of different textured images flipping like a slideshow through my mind. A white picket fence against a blue sky, butter dripping off corn on the cob, a sand dune, a small furry critter burrowing in the snow."

Do you prefer giving or receiving oral pleasure?

If you'd like to enjoy more mouth-to-Girl Boner pleasure, what steps could you or a partner take?

Exercise Seventeen

SEXY SPICE AND ECSTACY

"Only the united beat of sex and heart together can create ecstacy."
— Anaïs Nin, *Delta of Venus*

Describe a favorite sexual experience in as much detail as possible. What did you love most about it? What did it feel like physically?

What sexual experience do you hope to experience soon? Or someday?

Create a Sexy Play Bucket List.

Exercise Eighteen

CULTIVATING BODY-CONFIDENCE

"People always ask me, 'You have so much confidence. Where did that come from?' It came from me. One day I decided that I was beautiful, and so I carried out my life as if I was a beautiful girl . . . It doesn't have anything to do with how the world perceives you. What matters is what you see. Your body is your temple, it's your home, and you must decorate it."

—Gabourey Sidibe, actress

AT AGE THIRTY-TWO, IDAHO resident Amy Pence-Brown entered the words "why am I fat and happy" into a search engine, because she didn't know anyone who rejected cultural diet and beauty standards the way she did. The mother, writer, and artist has since become an advocate for shifting the ways we've been taught to perceive our bodies, frequently using her own body as a canvas for her art and activism.

Her most infamous performance to date, she said, involved stripping down to a black bikini and blindfold in the middle of a bustling Boise farmers market on a warm summer day in 2015. Clutching washable markers, she stood with a chalkboard at her feet, which read: "I'm standing for anyone who has struggled with a self-esteem issue like me, because all bodies are valuable. To support self-acceptance, draw a heart on my body."

"What resulted was the most beautiful and striking thing I've witnessed," she said of the experience. "A hidden photographer captured some images from the event and while right away you might notice my stretch marks, cellulite, sweat dripping down my back fat, silver hair, and sagging breasts that have nursed three babies in a wonky halter top, you can also see so much more than that. You can see the kindness, the humanity, and the acceptance [of passersby]."

If we don't decide to respect and see beauty in our bodies, society will fill in the gaps. And that is seldom pretty. Similar to embracing our sexuality, embracing our bodies can improve not only our own lives, but those of others. Every person who resists narrow and limiting definitions of beauty is an essential, world-improving role model. On the flip side, every time you shame your body or sexuality, you encourage others—especially the most vulnerable of people, such as kids—to shame theirs.

How do you feel about your body or appearance?

What influences in your life worsen your body image? What influences improve it?

Do you *want* to love your body? Why or why not?

Describe a time you felt gorgeous. How did it affect how you moved in the world?

Exercise Nineteen

BODY POSITIVITY & GIRL BONER BLISS

No matter your shape, size, gender, ethnicity, abilities, responsibilities, or age, you are worthy of pleasure.

———————————————

"LIGHT OFF, PLEASE" **MAY** not be most couples' idea of sex talk, but the phrase was nearly as commonplace in our sex life as kissing or touching. I'm not sure if my first boyfriend *ever* saw me fully naked. Instead, I found solace in darkness while concerns about my physique lingered until arousal swept me toward orgasm.

Once I began cultivating sexual empowerment, this completely changed. I no longer wished to starve the body I had newfound respect for or hide away in my cloak of darkness. While I still had my share of insecurities and a great deal to learn, I felt deeply worthy of pleasure. As a result, I began to better recognize and express my desires, move and even moan more freely, and allow my body to be seen as the pleasure-worthy wonder it was. Perhaps body respect is the best "foreplay" there is.

You don't have to "love your body" to have a fabulous sex life or invite Girl Boner bliss o' plenty. If you prioritize sexual pleasure, however, I can almost guarantee that your body image will improve in tandem.

How has your body image influenced your sex life?

How do you feel about your body during and after sex? Answer in general terms or choose a specific experience.

What would you like to improve in these areas?

Exercise Twenty

AGING BEAUTY

Beauty doesn't fade with age. It changes and deepens.

———————————

HAVE YOU EVER STOOD beside centuries-old trees? They bring a mix of comfort, respect, and awe. It's as though we can feel the hundreds of thousands of days they've seen and their will to inspire and protect. People travel across states and countries to admire their beauty.

As a culture, we celebrate the beauty of aging trees, fine wine, architecture, clothing, jewelry, and even furniture. Yet when we see an older person, particularly a woman, we're taught to see loss: loss of beauty, of youth, of sexuality. Aside from youth, none of those are actually lost. With years, we tend to gain experience, wisdom, skills, and self-confidence. And if fashion magazines and entertainment celebrated wrinkles and gray hair as the epitome of sexiness, we would all embrace aging with more gusto.

I've lost count of the number of women who've told me they began feeling invisible at a certain age. Here's to changing that, not only for ourselves, but for all women and femmes everywhere.

Observe people in their golden years. Journal about the beauty you see. If you don't see it straightaway, challenge yourself to think differently. Write about the experience.

How do you feel about your own aging process, whether you're now in your 20s, 40s, 50s, or beyond? What scares you? What feels luscious and divine?

How has the aging process influenced your sex life or desires around pleasure?

Describe the most beautiful older person you know. Write them a love letter.

Exercise Twenty-One

SEX AND STRESS

"Even if times are tough and you're enduring a terrible heartache, it's important to focus your anger on a vibrator, not another person."

—Chelsea Handler, *My Horizontal Life: A Collection of One Night Stands*

THERE WAS A TIME in sexuality and intimacy coach Natalie Hatjes' life when she didn't know who she was or who she aspired to be. The unknown felt scary, she said, and really stressed her out.

"I was an emotional eater so I filled my emptiness with chocolate, bread, and cheese . . . During this time between the poor body image, my unhealthy diet, and stress, my sex drive was slim to none. When I would have sex with my boyfriend, I would cry in middle of it," she said, adding that eventually, she realized how important it was to take care of herself; mind, body, and soul. "Crying during sex was my wakeup call to practice self care, change my diet, and exercise."

There's no such thing as a life without stress, but we can learn to better prevent and manage stressful happenings. While some folks cope with stress through sex and orgasm, stress is also a common libido tanker. Our bodies tend to tense up during stress, which doesn't make Girl Boners—or us—come easily. On top of that, it's not uncommon for people to feel stressed over not feeling "sexual enough" throughout stressful times, creating a frustrating double whammy.

It's perfectly fine to feel not so sex-inclined due to stress, which is a leading libido tanker for all genders. It's also okay, and potentially helpful, to prioritize sex as a stress-nuking therapy. For some people, stress revs their sexual engine as they crave medical, orgasmic release. Give yourself permission to feel these decisions out, one case at a time.

How does stress affect your Girl Boners or sex life?

Next time you feel ultra-stressed, consider solo play or another sensual activity, such as a sudsy bath. How did taking the time to intimately connect with yourself affect you?

Exercise Twenty-Two

SELF-CARE SUPREME

"Caring for myself is not self-indulgence, it is self-preservation, and that is an act of political warfare."

—Audre Lorde, civil rights activist, poet, and librarian

WHEN ACTOR AND WRITER Charlene Guzman was healing from sex and love addiction, self-care was vital, she told me during a *Girl Boner Radio* chat about the film she wrote and stars in, *Unlovable*.

"It was so interesting because much of my recovery was learning, what do I like to do? What feels good? What's my purpose? So to really explore that, so I made a list of everything I ever wanted to do but didn't," she said, adding that the list included going to puppet school and taking an aerial class, both of which she did. "Then nice things like buying myself flowers [and] taking baths. I had never done that ever before. I never did things that were nice for myself. It was always about some guy I was trying to impress."

All of that considered, it's not surprising that Charlene considers really showing up for and loving herself and choosing herself first her most cherished rewards.

"It's easy to do on the good days, but on the bad days, that's when the true test comes in—if can I love myself when it looks like this today," she said. "And I can now, where it's not life or death. I have the tools to take care of myself and get through it, and that is just amazing to me versus where I was five years ago."

Just as you are worthy of pleasure, you are worthy of supreme self-care, today and throughout your life. As basic and buzz word-y as it can seem, caring for ourselves must take priority in our lives. It's more than a practice; it's a basic human right.

Head to the self-care checklists in Chapter Nine of *Girl Boner*. Choose several items to prioritize this week, then write about your experience with each. (If you aren't able to purchase the book, email me at august@augustmclaughlin.com and I'll send you the checklists.)

Exercise Twenty-Three
BIRTH CONTROL DECISIONS

"No woman can call herself free who does not own and control her body. No woman can call herself free until she can choose consciously whether she will or will not be a mother."

—Margaret Sanger, birth control activist, sex educator, and nurse

———————————————

MARGARET SANGER WAS NOT without controversy, having been one of many people of the 1920s who believed in "selective mating" to improve the human race (a little too *Handmaid's Tale*, I know). But she also did a heck of a lot of good for vulva owners. She founded Planned Parenthood and spent time in jail for fighting for sex education and contraception rights.

"For me, Planned Parenthood was everything. It's where I got condoms and my first and only pelvic exams for a long time, as I couldn't afford to go anywhere else and did not have any health insurance," said Bethany M. of Albuquerque. "I've since been on various types of the pill and had weird side effects, so I switched to an IUD and love it. I think it's important to keep trying [birth control methods] out until you find one that works for you."

I wish everyone had the freedom to have children or not and to make choices around reproductive and sexual health. Whether you prefer natural methods of birth control, the pill, an IUD, condoms, or none at all, your choices are worthy and should always be your own.

Create a timeline of your birth control journey. What choices have you made and why? Describe your greatest birth control trials and triumphs.

If you're going through birth control changes now, use this space to track your experience, including pros and cons you notice along the way.

Exercise Twenty-Four
STIS AND SEXY SAFER SEX

Safer sex is a practice of self-love and mighty respect for others. So is de-stigmatizing sexually transmitted infections.

WHILE HER FEELINGS HAVE since shifted, Jenelle Marie Pierce considers learning she had herpes at age sixteen one of her most traumatic experiences. "I immediately believed herpes was a reflection of who I was: dirty, trashy, damaged-goods, slutty, tainted, nasty, disgusting, a monster, and being punished by God," she said. "It wasn't until years later I began to question the unreasonableness of those assumptions, because they didn't reflect how I felt about myself nor how anyone who loved me or cared for me felt."

Now the executive director of TheSTDProject.com and founder of the herpes activists network, HANDS, Jenelle wants anyone struggling as she once did to know that they are their own best advocate and that little does away with stigma better than empowering yourself with education and arming yourself with self-respect and self-love.

"I've learned that people are most afraid of what they don't understand," she said of navigating sex and STI status conversations post diagnosis. "We are taught to feel shame around a myriad of things, and the only way to move past shame and to a place of empowerment is to be as authentic as possible. When I discuss my status and why stigma is pervasive, I try my best to apply empathy."

Nearly everything pleasurable is risky in some way. Playing sports raises your risk for broken limbs. Driving a car can lead to fender benders. If you fall in love, you might experience heartbreak. That's why we have helmets, seat belts, friends, and therapy. And because sex is just as wondrous as your health and wellbeing, we have safer sex methods o' plenty. These practices can guard against STI transmission and make whatever sexual experiences you have more gratifying. If you end up with an infection regardless, as countless folks do at some point, know this: misconceptions around STIs are shameful, not you.

If you or a partner has had an STI, how did you find out? How did it make you feel?

What safer sex practices do you use?

How do you communicate about them? Jot down a sample conversation.

Describe a positive, or not-so-positive, experience you recall while navigating these issues. What did it teach you?

Exercise Twenty-Five
YOUR GORGEOUS IDENTITY

"We must abolish the entitlement that deludes us into believing that we have the right to make assumptions about people's identities and project those assumptions onto their genders and bodies."

—Janet Mock, *Redefining Realness: My Path to Womanhood, Identity, Love & So Much More*

BLOSSOM BROWN GREW UP in Jackson, Mississippi, a city known for southern hospitality, gospel soul music, and sumptuous soul food. It's not, however, known to be particularly trans-friendly. Assigned male at birth, she told me she came into her truth as a woman at age twenty-one.

Now an actress, producer, trans health advocate, and motivational speaker, Blossom appeared in *I Am Cait*, a documentary series that chronicled the life of Caitlyn Jenner, and on *The Ellen Degeneres Show*, after nursing schools rejected her for being trans. As her platform continues to grow, she uses it for good, educating others on a range of topics from the risks and challenges derived from transphobia to the beauty of embracing your authentic self and gender, however you define them.

"[Gender] is not just an outside feeling. It's how you feel on the inside as well," she said, pointing out that gender can be just as fluid as sexual orientation. "I think sometimes we forget about that. We're still so stuck on the whole binary—you're a man or you're a woman."

How do you identify in terms of sexual orientation and gender?

What pronouns do you prefer? She/her or he/him or something less binary, such as they/them or s/he and h/er?

Describe your sexuality using no gendered or sex-specific terms at all. Use colors, shapes, flavors, sensations, or whatever adjectives you please.

Exercise Twenty-Six
OF GOD(DESSES) AND GIRL BONERS

"I BEGAN TO LEAN into my desires as a queer woman," said Reverend Jes Kast. "And I thought, wait a minute. I have confidence in my faith, and I also trust the desires I have for women. And they might be holy and wonderful and wild all at the same time . . ."

This was a far cry from the purity culture she'd been a part of years prior which promoted abstinence from not only sex, but from sexual thoughts, touching, porn, and any other actions that might lead to sex.

Religious teachings underlie sexual shame for many people, especially women and people in the LGBTQIA+ community. But spirituality, sexuality, and yes, even religion, can work synergistically together, with each one fortifying the others. Most every religion encourages love, kindness, gratitude, and either meditation or prayer—mighty attributes that can add so much to your Girl Boner journey. If you're doubtful, review Chapter Thirteen in *Girl Boner*, which includes much more of Kast's journey.

What are your spiritual beliefs?

What religious teachings have interfered with your Girl Boner bliss?

If you're religious, what sex-positive messaging have you found within your faith community? If nothing comes to mind, what steps can you take to change that?

Exercise Twenty-Seven

PERMISSION TO WATCH
(OR NOT WATCH) PORN

"Porn exists in a parallel universe, a shadowy otherworld. When you force anything into the shadow and underground, you make it a lot easier for bad things to happen, and a lot harder for good things to happen."

—Cindy Gallop, founder of MakeLoveNotPorn

I HIT 'PLAY,' EXPECTING a rom-com. Instead, a voluptuous, naked woman appeared on the screen, moaning as she fondled her breasts and opened her legs as though prepping to swallow the camera. *Gulp*. I'd never seen porn before and there it was, spread eagle on my then boyfriend's TV. While I had been traveling and longing to be close to him, he'd been . . . occupied, it seemed. *Did he prefer those voluptuous bodies? Was I not enough?* On top of my insecurities, I'd absorbed messaging that porn is basically the devil incarnate, making matters even more complex. While I still don't rely on the medium, I see most-things-porn in a far different light.

Porn is another one of those elephants in the room. Although seldom discussed, most people have seen or have an opinion about it. Most "good girls" I've spoken to about porn learned it was dark, seedy, and best avoided. Some watch it anyway, with or without "I shouldn't be doing this" shame. Others who aren't hip on it for ethical reasons, stick to feminist porn for its greater inclusivity and less of the "male gaze," or prefer other tantalizing activities such as reading erotica.

My personal journey and countless porn-related conversations have taught me that more of us need to understand this: Watching porn doesn't make you an immoral "slut." *Not* watching porn doesn't make you an old-fashioned "prude." When porn enhances your sex life, relationships, and wellbeing, it's a groovy, embraceable practice. Equally valid is avoiding porn if it doesn't jive well with you for any reason. Only you can decide what works best for you and your relationship(s) at any given time.

How do you feel about porn? What led you to these feelings?

If you watch porn, how has it influenced your sex life?

If you don't watch porn, what sexually stimulating activities do you prefer instead? And why?

Exercise Twenty-Eight

SEX TOY MAGIC

"I urge you all today, especially today during these times of chaos and war, to love yourself without reservations and to love each other without restraint. Unless you're into leather."

—Margaret Cho, comedian, actress, and singer-songwriter

JOAN PRICE, AN ADVOCATE for ageless sexuality and author of several books about senior sex, including the award-winning *Naked at Our Age: Talking Out Loud about Senior Sex*, has been using vibrators since about 1975, when she purchased her first Magic Wand in the personal care department at Macy's.

"It was supposed relax sore muscles, but it was clear to me what part of my body it would 'relax,'" she said. "For decades, this vibrator and many others were my solo-sex companions. Later, as age decreased my hormones and my sexual responses, I discovered that a threesome consisting of me, my partner, and a favorite vibrator brought the zing back to my responsiveness and ensured orgasm. I learned to introduce my vibrators to new partners without embarrassment or apology. I also learned to pleasure my partners with them, too."

Now, at age seventy-five, Joan reviews sex toys "from a senior perspective" on her blog, aiming to spread the joy about the toys she sees more as 'orgasm tools.' "Some people my age think vibrator sex isn't 'natural,'" she offered. "If you love to dance but your knee doesn't work well anymore, you wouldn't hesitate to wear a knee brace, would you? You wouldn't forego reading glasses or cataract surgery if your eyes didn't work well 'naturally,' would you? Vibrators just help to keep our genitals working the way they're supposed to as we pile on the decades of life."

I think every orgasm-loving gal ought to have a treasure trove of Girl Boner goodies, and sex toys can make marvelous additions. They provide awesome ways to practice self-love and other-love, whether you decide to use them on your own or with a partner.

What sex toy(s) have you tried? Jot down a thought about each one.

Describe your favorite ways to use sex toys.

If you haven't yet tried a sex toy, which one might you try first? Examples of good starters include clitoral or G-spot vibrators, modest-size dildos, and cock rings.

Once you've purchased a new toy, write about your pre-play expectations, then describe the actual experience. How did your expectations and the results vary?

Exercise Twenty-Nine

QUICKIES VERSUS LONGIES

"Many lovers are 'off to the races': Hurtling towards orgasm, they miss the excitement of sensual meanderings along the way."

—Alexandra Katehakis, *Mirror of Intimacy: Daily Reflections on Emotional and Erotic Intelligence*

"I LOVE QUICKIES, I'D happily have them daily," said *Girl Boner* blog reader Jillian. "My boyfriend prefers to take his time, so much so that I end up feeling bored and impatient after I come."

"I have wished most of my partners would slow the F down," said another. "It takes me at least fifteen minutes to even start to feel ready for orgasm."

Both quickies and longies can be magical. (Okay, "longie" isn't actually a word, but you get the picture.) Delighting in some quickie fun because you love it, or rather than skipping sex because *who even has time?*, can go far in the intimacy and pleasure departments. Taking our time to savor sexual experiences rather than beelining toward orgasm every darn time can bring mighty benefits, too.

Do you prefer quickies, longies, or a mix of both?

Enjoy a quickie, alone or with a partner, when you'd normally skip it. Soon after, write about the experience. How did it feel to pause what you were doing and prioritize Girl Boner pleasure instead? Which parts of your body experienced pleasure?

Partake in some slow sexy playtime, alone or with a partner. Soon after, write about the experience. How did it feel to slow down? Which parts of your body experienced pleasure?

Exercise Thirty

KINKY ADVENTURES

"'Tie me up, please . . .' Chantal said. They looked above at some vines and roots hanging down from the grassy area above the depression in the canal they were standing in. She was in his hands—he had to comply. A little bit of kink was one of the most delicious of erotic pleasures."

—Jess C. Scott, *Catholic School Girls Rule*

"**THIS ONE MIGHT SOUND** cliché, but it was extremely hot for me and my partner," said Cam of Texas. "We are church-going, sexually vanilla people but one day after I had read a hot erotic story, I bought restraints . . . and we took turns tying each other up. The tied-up person wore a blindfold while the other went crazy with their mouth, lips, tongue . . . Just thinking about it now makes me excited. We decided to do it maybe once a year to keep it novel. It's so fun to look forward to."

Whether you're into BDSM-style kinkiness or not, most folks can benefit from bringing a sense of newness and adventure to sexy play. Getting busy in a unique place, trying new positions, role-playing, or even trying a new toy or masturbation style can fit the bill and bring big time rewards.

How do you define "kinky"?

Describe a kinky adventure you've fantasized about or experienced.

Describe another, and another.

Exercise Thirty-One
YES, NO, MAYBE LIST

FOR EACH ITEM, PLACE an X in the appropriate column: *Yes*, you're in! *No*, you're definitely not interested. *Maybe* you'd consider it at some point.*

	YES	NO	MAYBE
Anal sex			
Blindfolding			
Bondage (tying someone up/being tied up)			
"Dirty" talk			
Handcuffs			
Fisting (exactly what it sounds like!)			
Masochism (giving/receiving pleasure from pain)			
Mutual masturbation			
Orgasm control (getting close to orgasm, stopping, repeating)			

	YES	NO	MAYBE
Pegging (anal penetration with a strap-on)			
Role-playing			
Sadism (pleasure from humiliation)			
Spanking			
Temperature play (such as with warm water or ice cubes)			
Threesome or group sex			

*As you engage in any of these activities, remember to apply the pillars of BDSM, making it "safe, sane, and consensual."

Are there other or more specific activities that you would or wouldn't like to try?

Exercise Thirty-Two

MULTIPLE LOVES/LOVERS

"What I wish people understood is that polyamory is not the same as swinging. It is not about spicing up a relationship, or adding something [that's] missing. It is about love, not lust, not that there's anything wrong with lust. . . . Some of us are able to love more than one person at a time."

—Elizabeth M.

WE'VE ALL SEEN THE talk show episodes. Someone, typically a straight man, sits in the hot seat enduring questions about his multiple wives. Is he merely cheating? Is this some power trip to control and "keep" women? Or the result of an ultra-high libido?

While there are certainly abusive people who use unconventional relationship styles as tactics to abuse or control, they are the exception. (And, of course, plenty of abuse happens in monogamous pairings.) Many huge-hearted individuals prefer nontraditional relationships and partake in them privately, so as not to invite shaming from others.

If monogamy is not your thing, *that's 100 percent okay*. Go about non-monogamy ethically, being honest with yourself and your partners or lovers, knowing that your relationship choices are yours alone. No one has a right to tell you how to love.

If you're non-monogamous, how and when did you first realize it? What do you seek in a partner or lover? How do you navigate challenges, such as judgment from others who don't understand?

If you're monogamous, how can you better support people who aren't? What do you wish you understood about these types of relationships?

Exercise Thirty-Three

GIRL BONERS AND LOVE

"Love is a vessel that contains both security and adventure, and commitment offers one of the great luxuries of life: time. Marriage is not the end of romance, it is the beginning."

—Esther Perel, *Mating in Captivity: Reconciling the Erotic and the Domestic*

YOU COULD SAY IT started with me hunched over my stinky workout shoes. We were neighbors, had been spending time together as friends, and were about to go for a run together at a nearby park. Tying my shoes on his front steps, the same steps we'd first met on coincidentally, it hit me. Not, "I'm falling in love with this man," but, "OH MY GOD, I LOVE HIM."

While the *this is love* sureness seemed to happen in a single moment, it was really a culmination of many things: the kindness he showed to me and others, the easy way we could talk for hours, the magnetism in our then platonic hugs. The friendship with this man I was crazy about had been evolving into more, and that day I was ready to see it. Lucky for me, he'd noticed, too. We soon started dating, and a year and a half later, we were married on those steps. Ten years later, as #gross as it may sound, he still makes my heart flutter.

Falling in love is probably the most natural way to experience soul-shaking, zany-making intoxication. Staying in love can be intoxicating, too, in subtler, deeper, and more profound ways. And all nourishing relationships can benefit our Girl Boners.

Describe your ideal relationship. Include how you and partner(s) would make each other feel, the values you'd share, and possible adventures you'd cultivate.

If you have a partner, describe the day you met. How did you know this person was someone you wanted to share a relationship with?

How has a particular relationship helped you heal old wounds?

How do you express gratitude to your partner(s)?

What has heartbreak taught you?

Exercise Thirty-Four

PLEASURE AS A PRIORITY

"No woman gets an orgasm from shining the kitchen floor."
—Betty Friedan, author of *The Feminine Mystique*

(THOUGH I SUPPOSE IT depends on how you shine it!) Betty Friedan wrote the iconic bestseller *The Feminine Mystique* after a survey of her former classmates at Smith College showed high levels of dissatisfaction in their lives as 1950s housewives. While times have changed, the underlying issue of caring for others more than ourselves continues to interfere with orgasms. Caring for others is a *beautiful* thing. But when it interferes with your own self-care, including your sexual self-care (however you define that), it can work against you. When you prioritize your pleasure and wellbeing, on the other hand, you and your loved ones benefit.

I don't have kids, but I know from many friends, readers, listeners, and experts I've spoken to, as well as a fair amount of available research, that parenting can bring rich pleasure to parents' lives and challenges to the pleasure department, too.

"I didn't even realize I was doing it," Gita M. of Nevada told me. "I had a baby and then it was like, 'Okay! You're not a sexual person anymore. You have to be a 'proper mum.'" It took Gita a while to realize that she was investing so much time and energy into tending to the needs of everyone else in her life that her own pleasure was missing in (lack of) action. "One day my wife said to me, 'I miss your bliss, the X-rated kind,' and she missed my glow. She gave me a wrapped present, a new vibrator, and said,

'Can we put this on the to-do list?' . . . It just opened my eyes."

And by the way, she said yes, yes, yes. Not only to routine sexy play, but to keeping her personal pleasure in general on the radar. As a result, she said, she's a better parent.

Describe the latest happening(s) that have given you big-time pleasure.

What life demands tend to stand in the way of your orgasms or other types of personal pleasure?

How do you prioritize pleasure, especially during hectic times? If you tend not to, how could you turn this around?

Exercise Thirty-Five

SEX FREQUENCY—HOW OFTEN IS NORMAL?

"MY PARTNER AND I have sex once every month or two. *Is that normal?*"

"I use my vibrator a few times a week. *Is that normal?*"

"How often should a couple who's been together for a while be having sex?" (Put another way, *"Are we normal?"*)

I hear variations of these questions often. "Normal" is a wacky word, in the context of sex and sexuality. Sex isn't like body temperature, where most everyone should meet a basic standard. There's only what feels ideal to you at any given time. It's natural to desire and engage in more sexy play at certain times and less at others, regardless of your gender, genitalia, or relationship status.

If you sense room for improvement in this area, dig deeper, starting with this question: How do you define sex? (Are you concerned that you engage in naked-partner-play too seldom or frequently? Is it intercourse, anything-orgasmic, or some other definition you're concerned about?)

If you're concerned about your sex frequency, why do think that is?

What would you like to see change in this area? How can you cultivate such changes?

If you're content with your sex frequency but feel "abnormal" anyway, can you pinpoint when and how you developed that impression? What do you think would happen if you stopped shaming yourself for it? How could you best get there?

Exercise Thirty-Six
GIRL BONER ETHICS

"Faithfulness is about honoring your commitments and respecting your friends and lovers, about caring for their well-being as well as your own."

—Dossie Easton, *The Ethical Slut: A Guide to Infinite Sexual Possibilities*

ONE THING I KNOW about "good girls" is that guiding by our values ranks high on our must-do lists. This can feel challenging when our values shift or misalign with those of others or clash against beliefs instilled in you since you were a child. When the old tapes take over or someone judges you harshly, remind yourself of this: Your value system is valid, no matter how you define it today, tomorrow, or ten years from now.

After Angelique Luna's value system was challenged in a hurtful way, she turned the experience into activism. Engaged in the swinging lifestyle since her late teens, she says she enjoys playing with a couple as long as they've been together for over a year. In the swinging community she met her husband who, like her, identifies as bisexual.

"We went on a date with a couple and they demanded that I go down on the woman. I said no [because] I do not enjoy going down on a woman. I will kiss her on the lips, caress her body, and play with toys. That is what I enjoy with women."

Angelique had every right to uphold her wishes, yet after the incident rumors spread that Angelique was only pretending to be bisexual to be part of the swinging community. Angered that people were not respecting her sexual activity choices, she launched a blog that would become a podcast called Living a Sex Positive Life, with the aim of "educating the world that there are more flavors of sex."

   To anyone feeling wobbly about upholding their own non-negotiables, Angelique suggests this: "Honor yourself. It sucks to be alone, but you will find your tribe. Remember you are not everyone's cup of tea." No one is, nor does anyone need to be. Be your own special brew and protect it, knowing that rewards of many kinds will follow.

   What are your non-negotiables around sex and relationships?

   Describe your relationship values. Why is each one important to you?

   Do you embrace and stand strong in your values? If not, what's holding you back?

Exercise Thirty-Seven

~~SORRY~~ NOT SORRY

That thing you keep apologizing for? It might actually be your superpower.

HOW OFTEN DO YOU apologize? I'm not talking about the genuine "I'm so sorry that happened to you" type remarks, or the sorries you offer when you've hurt someone and regret it. I'm talking about self-shaming and self-blaming when little, if any, apology is due.

Femmes in particular tend to over-apologize. And "good girls?" We are the *worst*. But it's not our fault. (Let's not apologize for over-apologizing.) Being perceived as impolite or bothersome can seem abhorrent to those of us who've absorbed the notion that to be "good," we must behave in "acceptable" ways—which, for gals, tends to mean demure, polite, and not bothersome. "I'm so sorry, but I'm actually allergic to a food in this dish," we might say to a server who mistook our order. Or, "I'm really sorry, but I'm actually already seeing someone," to someone who requests our phone number.

Common examples of undue apologies I've observed:
    For being too loud, assertive, or inquisitive
    For being too quiet or introverted
    For canceling plans due to feeling overwhelmed, overworked, or sleep-deprived
    For taking time for ourselves
    For being a morning person or night owl
    For expressing our true feelings

For talking for more than a few seconds
For requesting a clarification
For feeling too sad, frustrated, anxious, or enthusiastic
For taking up space

It breaks my heart that so many of these, and many other examples, involve attributes and precious parts of who we authentically are. Gorgeous transformations can ignite when we catch ourselves needlessly apologizing and shift away from our "I'm so sorry (for being me)" behaviors.

What do you tend to over-apologize for? Observe your interactions with people for a few days, taking note of every instance or urge.

What do you apologize for that's actually one of your strengths?

Exercise Thirty-Eight
WHEN YOU FEEL LIKE TOO MUCH

"**AS IT TURNS OUT**, being quirky and precocious wasn't a great way to make friends in elementary school," said joy expert, Maya Hampton—at least, it wasn't for her. Often deemed too smart or pretty, boys grabbed at her, accusing her of thinking herself superior to others.

"In college and the workplace, the commentary changed but the criticism remained," she said. "Now when I give my analysis of a book I'm reading or a geopolitical event, I'm accused of being intimidating. Women and men audibly marvel that I'm married. They say, 'Wow, he must be quite a guy to be able to handle you'... If I share that I'm autistic, I'm barraged with another assortment of insults."

While she used to be confused by these reactions, the joy expert now sees people's pain, insecurities, and judgments behind them and wants to show people that self-hate isn't an edifying pastime, adding that "self-worth is innate, and it's important not to let social criticism convince you otherwise."

Go back to the last section and notice how many of your undue apologies involve being "too much." Pretty striking, right? I call the state of feeling as though we're excessive when we're simply being ourselves "toomuchiness." It's how you feel after sending an email you feel desperate to un-send out of fear you were too wordy or demanding, or when you're moved to tears and then apologize for being "too emotional."

Often, at its core, toomuchiness involves the opposite: a sense of insufficiency. "I'm too much of a prude" could actually mean "I'm not sexy/

sensual enough." "I'm too quiet" could reflect shame around not being extroverted when you're by nature a beautiful introvert.

No matter how you experience these feelings, start trading them for self-compassion. Give yourself some grace. Every time you allow yourself to be unapologetically yourself, you free up more of your magic to share with the world. There is no such thing as too much of you.

When do you feel like too much? List some examples.

For each item above, jot down a reason you're in fact *not* too much.

What person/people do you admire who seem unabashedly themselves?

Exercise Thirty-Nine
DEALING WITH DIFFICULT FEELINGS

"If we learn to open our hearts, anyone, including the people who drive us crazy, can be our teacher."

—Pema Chödrön, *When Things Fall Apart: Heart Advice for Difficult Times*

SOME YEARS AGO, I began slipping into a dark space I hadn't seen in years. I'd stopped taking a medication I rely on, having convinced myself I'd meditated away need for it and perhaps having absorbed some of the stigma that's so pervasive in our culture. When, after months of increasing challenges, other stressors cropped up, it was though I was losing my last bit of power in a storm. The darkness became all-encompassing and for a while, I feared I might never climb out. Virtually nothing brought me pleasure, which was a huge red flag that finally led me to seek support.

Rather than accept my feelings as they lingered longer than I decided they "should," even after I'd sought help, I shamed myself for them: *Why are my feelings such a problem?* Which turned into renditions of *Why am I such a problem?* Why couldn't I just deal? Then one day, after I'd finally found support, someone gave me the permission I hadn't realized I needed. "You are allowed to have these feelings longer than you'd like," she said, adding that healing has no time limit.

When it comes to painful emotions, the only way up is through. Sometimes simply *feeling the feelings* we desperately want to "fix" *is* the fix. Sometimes it's the most proactive thing, especially when it's also the most painful. If we resist or bully our emotions, they can become a crisis of their own, standing in the way of pleasure and our overall wellbeing. But if we feel them with all our might, well, there's magic there.

How do you deal with difficult feelings when they crop up?

How has stifling or allowing for these feelings impacted pleasure in your life?

Exercise Forty

SEXY ZEN

"Great sex is sheer abandonment, letting go of inhibition and self-consciousness, and giving in to the heat of the moment."

—Philip Toshio Sudo, *Zen Sex: The Way of Making Love*

———————————

"I HAVE OCD, ANXIETY, and ADHD, so you can imagine how easily meditation does *not* come for me," said Helen, an artist and entrepreneur in South Beach Miami.

For years, Helen's symptoms interfered with sex and dating, to the point that she figured she would remain single indefinitely. And while she enjoyed single-hood, she longed to share the "ins and outs of life" with a partner. "On top of that," she added, "my sexual needs were only met by my hand or vibrator, as I am not someone who enjoys casual sex."

Therapy, lifestyle changes, and finding the right medication all helped, and she ended up meeting RJ, a kind, sensitive guy who made her laugh from the get-go: "He tells the dorkiest jokes, but they're so bad it makes them funny."

"I was really nervous about the sex part, but more orgasms turned out to be what was missing from my treatment regime," she recalled. "Not that it's *treatment*, per say, but you know what I mean? It's practically the only time my mind settles down."

Raise your hand if you can relate to this to some degree. While it's completely normal and okay to have a swirl of thoughts during sex (and you can still experience pleasure meanwhile), I'm not sure there's anything in this world as present-bringing as orgasm. There's often a luscious moment during sex when your desire takes fully over and the entire world seems to disappear.

What lessons have sex and orgasm taught you about mindfulness?

How do you bring yourself into the here and now? How do you, or could you, practice mindfulness?

How does it benefit your sex life or relationships?

Exercise Forty-One
STRENGTH IN FEMININITY

"In a world where masculinity is respected and femininity is regularly dismissed, it takes an enormous amount of strength and confidence for any person, whether female- or male-bodied, to embrace their feminine self."

—Julia Serano, PhD, *Whipping Girl: A Transsexual Woman on Sexism and the Scapegoating of Femininity*

I met a woman recently who has two transgender kids, one male and one female. When the boy, assigned female at birth, first began his transition, he stopped playing with dolls for a while. When the girl, assigned male at birth, began hers, she put sports she loved aside. It was as though they wanted to make sure everyone around them accepted them for who they truly are, their mother said. Society says girls love pink, and dolls, and dress-up. Boys are supposed to love blue, and trucks, and baseball. As they gained acceptance from others, both children reclaimed their previous hobbies—and neither were less "female" or "male" because of it.

Gender is an identity, not ruled by colors, hobbies, fantasies, or desires. However you choose to express yours is valid.

What about you feels feminine?

Describe your seemingly masculine traits.

How do you embrace both parts of yourself, and everything in between? How do they impact your sexuality?

Exercise Forty-Two
SEX AND AUTHENTICITY

"If you trade your authenticity for safety, you may experience the following: anxiety, depression, eating disorders, addiction, rage, blame, resentment, and inexplicable grief."

—Brené Brown, *The Gifts of Imperfection: Let Go of Who You Think You're Supposed to Be and Embrace Who You Are*

———————

WHEN WE EMBRACE OUR sexual desires and preferences rather than attempt to fit a mold that Society, the Patriarchy, or Fill-in-the-Blank told us "good girls" should aspire to, all facets of our lives suffer. Thankfully, the opposite is also true: When we embrace our sexuality, in all its fullness, our entire lives benefit. We're less inclined to cling to relationships or pursuits that hurt us, shrink away when courage is due, or stifle our natural appetites. We find passions and talents we might never have otherwise discovered. We attract relationships that nourish, rather than diminish, us. And while embracing one's sexuality is by no means a cure for mental illness, it can support us through those journeys as well.

One might think that Mona Darling already fully embraced her truest sexual desires once she began working as a dominatrix. But as her experience shows, even well into our sexual empowerment journeys we can meet chances to fine tune.

She entered the work with a lot of expectations about the behaviors, look, and disposition of a dominatrix. And for the first year or so, she worked hard to fit that mold. "I tried to be mean, and heartless even," she recalled. "I tried to be cold and uncaring, aloof, and impeccably dressed in black shiny fetish wear. But this is not me."

Sure, she has a thing for "the black and shiny," but she also loves vintage girdles, cosplay, and feminine cloths. And having met Mona multiple times, I can assure you there's not a mean bone in her body. (No pun intended?) Figuring she couldn't be a dominatrix without morphing into the Cruella she wasn't, she told herself that eventually she'd do so if she just kept at it. But . . . that didn't happen. Instead, she was too busy stressing to have any fun with her clients, who she believes sensed the falsity.

Eventually, she allowed herself to unclench enough to be herself with one or two clients, she said, her "goofy, pun-filled, giggling, silly costumed self" who was into the "weird stuff," such as crossdressing and humiliation, and who cared deeply for her clients, even as she consensually hurt them. The one who would giggle about a run in her stockings she noticed mid-session.

"Coming to this realization made me realize that when I'm goofball myself, I'm happier, and I attract the people that appreciate me, inside the dungeon/bedroom, and outside of it," she said. If you're struggling to step into your truest sexual desires, consider Mona's advice: "Realize that there are people out there that are just as weird and interested in the kinky weird stuff. And maybe if you put yourself out there, you will find them."

What sexual activity have you long wanted to try, but haven't? What's holding you back?

When do you feel the most authentic? Or the least like yourself?

If you were to live or love more authentically, describe a typical day or evening:

Exercise Forty-Three
NURTURING INDEPENDENCE

"Transformation doesn't ask that you stop being you. It demands that you find a way back to the authenticity and strength that's already inside of you. You only have to bloom."

—Cheryl Strayed, *Brave Enough*

YOU KNOW WHAT'S DIFFICULT? Feeling afraid to be alone. Ironically, that's often the best time to nurture independence. It's easy to look outside of ourselves for someone or something to "fix" or "complete" us when we're struggling. While we all lean on others for support, there's a big difference between seeking support and attempting to fill a void or distract ourselves from uncomfortable feelings by way of a new relationship, frenetic schedules, or self-harm.

Every aspect of our lives benefits from bringing a whole, embraced self to the mix, including our sex lives and capacity for pleasure. A partner or lover might help us through difficult or insecure times (the best ones do), but not because we're somehow broken or insufficient. You're already whole and enough on your own. Water that garden like an ocean.

I've encountered few people who've done such "watering" as powerfully as M, a screenwriter whose (now ex) husband revealed his sex addiction—which he used to justify rampant deceit and infidelities—on her thirty-eighth birthday. After they parted, she landed in a turbulent rebound relationship and more chaos no one should have to endure. By the time we met, M seemed fully on her own two feet. But as you might guess, the path there has been far from easy.

"I searched for answers everywhere—the internet, books, almost everyone I met," she said. Why had these things happened to her? Finally, a trauma therapist allowed her to openly hurt in sessions devoid of judgment. She encouraged M to make new friends, assuring her that another person's poor behavior was not her fault and that trust, honesty, and vulnerability are essential for healthy relationships.

M realized that in order to trust others again, she would have to rebuild trust in herself. She moved across the country and committed to her dream screenwriting career. Meanwhile, she didn't date and barely moved her body, skipping everything from exercise to sex, even solo-style; her body and soul had been through too much. After progress that included moving into her own apartment and selling her first script, she longed to "re-inhabit her body."

"I knew I wanted to feel my body again, but it was in turmoil, roiling with indigestion and falling into sluggish stupors after eating," she said. "Finally I was diagnosed with type 2 diabetes. My hand was forced. My first reaction was fury at my ex: *If only he hadn't been such a wretched human being, I'd never have abused my own body this way* . . . So back into therapy I went. A dear nutritionist friend coached me lovingly, and after the initial shock and a couple of therapy sessions, I realized all I wanted to do was take back control of myself fully. I now love taking daily walks, jazzercizing with the seniors at my local Y, and eating in ways that fill my soul."

M's Girl Boner has benefited from her efforts as well—as she put it, "and HOW!" "Even my fantasies now include new scenarios, new faces, [and] new desires. Sure, the old ones still wander around in there, but whatever I feel is mine. I date now and then, although I'm far pickier these days about who I invest time in . . . I'd love to find a regular partner again someday, but honestly, I've never felt better about myself than I do now as a single woman."

How do you nurture your personal wants, dreams, or passions?

How does doing so, or *not* doing so, impact pleasure in your life?

If you haven't been feeling independent and wish to be, what steps can you take to start adjusting that?

Exercise Forty-Four

YOU'RE MUCH MORE THAN
HOW MUCH YOU ACCOMPLISH

"When we work with love, we renew the spirit; that renewal is an act of self-love, it nurtures our growth. It's not what you do, but how you do it."

—bell hooks, *All About Love*

EARLIER THIS YEAR, RAYNE Parvis realized that most of her thoughts involved social media and ways to further her productivity and success as a personal stylist in Los Angeles. "I would meet a friend for dinner and think, 'Oh, I should get a photo for social media so I could do two things at once,'" she said. "I wasn't just having a night out with my friends. I was doing something 'productive,' too, which made me feel less guilty . . . My entire life was affected by my need to constantly do."

Rather than relax while watching TV with her husband, she'd post on social media so she wouldn't feel like "a lazy lady." And during meaningful conversations with loved ones, her thoughts scrolled her to-do list. So she took action of another kind: a thirty-day break from social media she now calls "the best thing ever."

"You don't realize how much seeing what other people are posting creeps into your own life, or how so-and-so had this happen to them and why has nothing amazing happened to you on your end?" she said of the lessons. "During the thirty days, I was able to focus more, feel grateful for my little baby step accomplishments, and enjoy leisure activities without distractions. I set times to work on my business and got back to being in the moment. When you're not comparing yourself to people or having the need to do anything it's amazing how much better you feel about yourself and your surroundings."

Now that she's back on social media, Rayne feels less obligated to endlessly engage, having learned that the world and her to-do list aren't going anywhere. "It's all about balance," she said. "Going overboard can still be tempting, but your mind needs time to chill. Now my walks in nature are sweeter, the house chores get done faster, movies are better, and conversations with friends and family are more memorable."

We live in a culture in which hyper-productivity and even stress are frequently boasted about: *Can you believe I haven't eaten all day? Who has time for sleep?!?* A day off—what's that?" Translation: "I'm so productive!" But there's a lot more to praise about not overextending ourselves, setting strengthening boundaries, and prioritizing practical self-care, even if it isn't Instagram-friendly. Sometimes the most proactive thing we can do is rest for the sake of it. Don't allow yourself to grow so busy being "productive" or comparing yourself to others that life's gifts pass you by.

When do you tend to compare yourself to others or their accomplishments?

Are you missing out on pleasure because of these feelings or your reactions? If so, how?

Jot down specific jealous or comparative thoughts you tend to have and more positive, pleasure-centric alternatives you could aim for.

Exercise Forty-Five
THE POWER OF PLAY

WHEN I THINK OF play, Kait Scalisi, MPH comes to mind. I met the big-hearted sex educator and founder of Passion by Kait through a blogging conference where she was moving through crowds with Vicky, her vulva puppet. (Obviously, we needed to be friends.) She's someone who will dance in public simply because she feels moved, and whose date adventures with her long-time partner inspire many to find #FreedominPleasure. But that's not all she shares. Kait speaks vulnerably and openly of her personal struggles. So I wasn't surprised when her response to my questions about playfulness included some of each.

Near the end of 2014, she told me, her relationship was in a tough spot. She and her partner had started a vacation with a "Big Scary Talk," involving the state of their relationship: *Where would they go from here?*

"Thankfully, we were on a hiking trip with lots of opportunities to play, explore, and try new things together," she said. "We laughed at my scaredy-catness over nature, pushed each other to climb higher and conquer fears, and stood in awe of the Grand Canyon's beauty. These acts reminded us of our connection, even if mentally and emotionally we were still working through conflict. We hear a lot about how thoughts influence actions, but the opposite is true too: How you act influences your thoughts and emotions."

The same attitude that drew them closer then makes what could be moment-breakers (examples she shared included farting during oral sex or a hip popping out of its socket at the moment of orgasm) an opportunity for more fun. A ruined moment has become a foreign concept, she said, "because we feel the mortification, laugh about the awkward moment, and get back to finding freedom in pleasure with each other."

It's easy to get so focused on trials at hand or getting things done that we scarcely have time for pleasure. Even if you adore your busy-makers, they can become crazy-makers if you seldom make time for anything else. And as Kait and her beau demonstrate often, a difficult time doesn't have to mean a full-on pause on fun. Play is a powerful balm for the soul that can benefit everything from our energy levels and moods to our relationships and sexual health. If you value your wellbeing enough to schedule annual physicals and brush your teeth twice a day, rank playfulness and pleasure highly, too.

What are your favorite ways to play?

How can you bring more playfulness into your sex life or relationships?

Exercise Forty-Six

SETTING BOUNDARIES

"We need to be inundating these children with the idea that consent is the way of life. Yes, you do have to ask to touch somebody."

—Tarana Burke, civil rights activist and founder of the Me Too movement

---

AFTER HER DAUGHTER MARCIA caught the brunt of "mean girl" middle school behavior, Lanae St. John, a sexologist and coach in California, asked her how she would apply lessons she learned from the experience to dating, once she started.

"If someone tries to put me down, I'll know that I am awesome," Marcia replied. "It's not a good use of my time to spend it with people who don't notice that I'm there or care that I'm there. That will help me in the long run because I'll be able to choose my friends more wisely."

This kid was in *seventh grade*.

While blown away by her daughter's confidence and boundary-setting skills, she wasn't entirely surprised. Having grown up Catholic, "with all the requisite fear, shame, and guilt," Lanae's efforts to instill these attributes has been very intentional. "I want my kids to know they can say no, hold boundaries for what they do and don't want, and know their own pleasure before they expect a partner to 'teach' or show them," she said.

Boundaries and consent involve so much more than "yes" or "no," and go well beyond romantic and sexual interactions. You've probably heard some rendition of "Saying yes to one thing says no to something else," and vice versa. If you agree to attend an event when you're completely wiped out, you could be saying no to your health and wellbeing, and so on. Setting boundaries takes this strengthening practice further. Before you even reach a yes or no question, you can rest easy, knowing your limitations are set.

When you encounter an acquaintance, do you prefer a hug, handshake, or neither?

When do you definitely *not* want hugs, kisses, or other touch?

How can you better respect these preferences—as well as those of others?

Describe a boundary you've set lately. How helpful has it been?

What boundary could you stand to set for a more vibrant existence?

Exercise Forty-Seven

AROUSING YOUR LIFE

"Life is either a great adventure or nothing."
—Helen Keller, *Let Us Have Faith*

A FEW YEARS AGO I woke up the morning after a tech-free vacation and, as per non-vacation usual, immediately checked my email. I soon noticed a slump in my energy, which lingered throughout the day. While vacationing, I'd spent my awakening moments outside, sipping tea as I observed the sunrise. There was nothing stopping me from doing the same at home, so why hadn't I? Ever since, I've aimed to ease into most days, and I can't believe the difference it makes. While I still fall into over-seriousness, overwork, and letting Ms. Pleasure grow dusty in a corner at times, whenever I start the day with personal time, I feel more alive and centered moving forward. The perks seems to sprinkle over dang near everything I do and every interaction I have that day.

As I shared in *Girl Boner*, I consider this practice of tapping into our pleasure centers and aiming to really connect with ourselves the most powerful form of "foreplay." The more we nurture that which brings us even small snippets of joy, the richer and more authentic our experiences will be—all-things-Girl Boner included. It's the surest way to arouse our whole lives.

What vacation-like practice could you incorporate into your life?

What area of your life could benefit from more adventure?

Describe an adventure you've cherished for each of the following categories:

Daily life

Wellness/self-care

Dating/romance

Sex

Friendships

Place a star next to items you could enjoy again.

Exercise Forty-Eight
A BEAUTIFUL BEGINNING

"I'M NOT INTERESTED IN a smorgasbord of men." When my mom spoke these words to my dad when they started dating, she feared he would run away. They were only nineteen and twenty-one, after all, and "what young man wants to hear that?" She wanted a committed partnership with someone with whom she could build a family and figured supreme honesty was the best way to avoid a spree of meaningless dates and relationships. (Side note, she's also a bit of a blurter.)

He not only stayed, but expressed similar goals and asked if she'd read a book he appreciated about raising children to be their own individuals—a philosophy that would set the tone for my and my siblings' lives. In barely two dates, their lives apart ended and a grand new adventure had begun.

My favorite stories end with a beginning: lovers finally uniting, an illness being cured, someone who struggled deeply finding their tremendous wings. Your Girl Boner journey is no different. *Thank you* for being one of my favorite stories. May your path, and your Girl Boner, continue to delight and surprise you in countless magnificent ways.

Reflect back on your Girl Boner journey and the efforts you've invested to this point. What changes have you noticed?

What efforts have you found most challenging?

What have been the juiciest rewards?

What would you like to cultivate or work on as your Girl Boner journey continues?

Further Reading

The Sex & Pleasure Book: Good Vibrations Guide to Great Sex for Everyone by Carol Queen, PhD and Shar Rednour

What's Up Down There? Questions You'd Only Ask Your Gynecologist If She Was Your Best Friend by Lissa Rankin, MD

Mating in Captivity: Unlocking Erotic Intelligence by Esther Perel

What Do Women Want? Adventures in the Science of Female Desire by Daniel Bergner

Brave Enough by Cheryl Strayed

Girl Boner: The Good Girl's Guide to Sexual Empowerment by August McLaughlin

About the Author

AUGUST MCLAUGHLIN is a nationally-recognized health and sexuality writer, media personality, and creator of Girl Boner®. Her podcast, *Girl Boner Radio*, reaches thousands of listeners every month and her articles have appeared in *Cosmopolitan, DAME Magazine, HuffPost, The Good Men Project*, and more. A frequent speaker on women, sexuality, and gender equality issues, McLaughlin has been a featured TEDx presenter and attended the United State of Women summit, convened by the White House, as a nominated change maker.

INDEX TO ENTRIES

INTRODUCTION
The Thing About Soul Truths 1
How to use this book 6

EXERCISE ONE
Starting Where You Are 11

EXERCISE TWO
Recalling Sex Ed 15

EXERCISE THREE
Real Talk About Periods 18

EXERCISE FOUR
Girl Boner Turning Points 21

EXERCISE FIVE
When The Truth Hurts 24

EXERCISE SIX
Your Sexy Parts 27

EXERCISE SEVEN
Ode to Your Genitals 31

EXERCISE EIGHT
Permission to Want 35

EXERCISE NINE
Mismatched Libidos 39

EXERCISE TEN
Titillating Turn-Ons 42

EXERCISE ELEVEN
Choosing Your Turn-Ons 45

EXERCISE TWELVE
Girl Boner Buzzkills 49

EXERCISE THIRTEEN
Your Body, Turned On 53

EXERCISE FOURTEEN
Different Types of 'Gasms 57

EXERCISE FIFTEEN
Sexy Solo Play 61

EXERCISE SIXTEEN
Oral Sex Sexiness 65

EXERCISE SEVENTEEN
Sexy Spice and Ecstacy 68

EXERCISE EIGHTEEN
Cultivating Body-Confidence 71

EXERCISE NINETEEN
Body Positivity & Girl Boner Bliss 75

EXERCISE TWENTY
Aging Beauty 78

EXERCISE TWENTY-ONE
Sex and Stress 81

EXERCISE TWENTY-TWO
Self-Care Supreme 85

EXERCISE TWENTY-THREE
Birth Control Decisions 89

EXERCISE TWENTY-FOUR
STIs and Sexy Safer Sex 93

EXERCISE TWENTY-FIVE
Your Gorgeous Identity 97

EXERCISE TWENTY-SIX
Of God(desses) and Girl Boners 101

EXERCISE TWENTY-SEVEN
Permission to Watch (Or Not Watch) Porn 104

EXERCISE TWENTY-EIGHT
Sex Toy Magic..107

EXERCISE TWENTY-NINE
Quickies Versus Longies.......................................112

EXERCISE THIRTY
Kinky Adventures..115

EXERCISE THIRTY-ONE
Yes, No, Maybe List..118

EXERCISE THIRTY-TWO
Multiple Loves/Lovers..120

EXERCISE THIRTY-THREE
Girl Boners and Love..123

EXERCISE THIRTY-FOUR
Pleasure as a Priority..126

EXERCISE THIRTY-FIVE
Sex Frequency—How Often is Normal?...............129

EXERCISE THIRTY-SIX
Girl Boner Ethics..132

EXERCISE THIRTY-SEVEN
~~Sorry~~ Not Sorry...135

EXERCISE THIRTY-EIGHT
When You Feel Like Too Much.............................139

EXERCISE THIRTY-NINE
Dealing with Difficult Feelings.............................143

EXERCISE FORTY
Sexy Zen..147

EXERCISE FORTY-ONE
Strength in Femininity..151

EXERCISE FORTY-TWO
Sex and Authenticity..154

EXERCISE FORTY-THREE
Nurturing Independence --158

EXERCISE FORTY-FOUR
You're Much More Than How Much You Accomplish --------------162

EXERCISE FORTY-FIVE
The Power of Play --165

EXERCISE FORTY-SIX
Setting Boundaries --168

EXERCISE FORTY-SEVEN
Arousing Your Life --172

EXERCISE FORTY-EIGHT
A Beautiful Beginning --177